The Grassington...

to

West Coast

Walk

written &

researched

by

John White

Fractal Press

Cover by BoE Design.

Maps: Reproduced by permission of Ordnance Survey
on behalf of HMSO © Crown Copyright 2007. All
rights reserved. Ordnance Survey Licence number:
100038371

British Library Cataloguing in Publication Data
A catalogue record of this book is available from the
British Library.

ISBN: 978-1-870735-35-3

Introduction

Welcome to the second long distance walk that makes its start from the village of Grassington. The first walk from Grassington to Robin Hood's Bay takes full advantage of the position of Grassington right in the middle of the country. The East Coast Walk follows a route through really wonderful country including two National Parks to a stunning, rugged coastline.

This walk, to the West Coast, does the same but with some major differences that make it a really special experience. The first difference, walking west, is that all the southern edge of the Dales lies before us. This includes some of the most famous and attractive features in the whole of the National Park - Malham Cove, Gordale Scar, Warrendale Knots, Ingleborough, and some nice little Caves. Beyond that is country that is not in a National Park, but probably should be. It is a walker's joy, wonderful to walk through and discover what lies beyond the views from the road.

As well as the gem of limestone around Hutton Roof & Farleton Fell, and the beautiful paths that seem to carry you effortlessly through the woods around Silverdale and Arnside, there is the coast itself. If you go looking for another rugged coastline, like on the east coast, there is a danger of missing the genuine beauty of this side of the country. This is a big sky landscape, which has its own mystery on a grey day and bursts through and dazzles at the slightest hint of light from the sky. The long finale of this walk West takes three days, during which you are always close to the coast, with the Sea, the Sky and the vast openness of Morecambe Bay for company.

I should mention that, although I have described this walk over seven (or eight) days, it is quite easy to split a couple of the days into shorter walks, especially the first two which visit so many places of interest they could be allowed to fill four days just by themselves.

This is an adventure that crosses a vast space to the open sky and incandescent light of the West Coast.

I hope you get there and enjoy getting there.

The following pages describe the route for each day in more detail. The description breaks the walk up into a number of sections between 'Waypoints' which are usually placed at natural turns or important places. I have not mentioned every stile or field that has to be crossed. Instead, I have included the best Ordnance Survey maps - 1:25000 (2½ inches to the mile) which show every track and all field boundaries. The best advise for following the guide is to trust the map first and use the instructions to clarify anything that is not immediately obvious. The arrows on the map show the route for each day, with different coloured arrows where there are alternatives. The Waypoint numbers also appear on the map as small coloured rectangles with the number in white - e.g.

WP22   WP22

so you can identify the nearest waypoint from the map and then follow the directions in the text as well as the arrows. The distance to the next waypoint should help you to pace your walk for the greatest comfort as well as knowing when to anticipate the next turn. The altitude data, on the first page of each chapter is intended to help you anticipate the effort that will be required each day. Don't be put off by the altitude graphs, they are exaggerated to produce a profile of hills, not mountains and the highest is 2400 ft - if it was produced to scale across 100 miles it would be little more than a flat line.

Although large scale map extracts are included, and in the previous book I thought that was enough, I have been persuaded that having the maps may help to identify parts of the larger landscape. Explorer series Maps OL2, OL6, OL7 cover the complete walk at 1:25000 scale.

Table of Contents

Large Scale Maps

Photographs

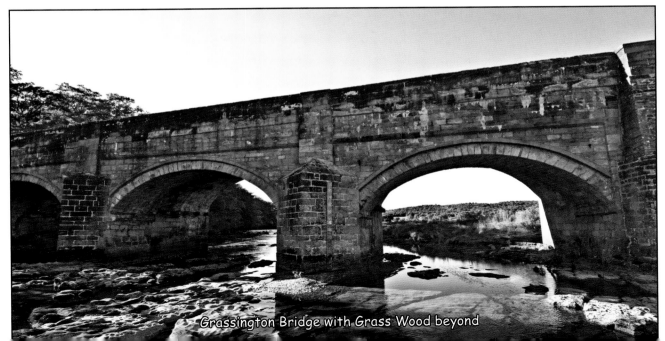

Grassington Bridge with Grass Wood beyond

Preparation

The Walk West is a genuine challenge for most walkers. The first three days require you to walk quite a few miles and climb a number of reasonable hills. Although there are many people who could try to complete it in a few of days, my opinion is that much more pleasure can be gained by taking your time. The first two days can easily be split into four, all of which will be a pleasure in themselves.

Apart from trying not to rush, there are a few other things that will add to the experience.

The first is to carry as little as possible. Some of things that you should take are quite obvious but I will mention them anyway - blister pads. I haven't had a walking blister for a few years but it is good to know that I have these useful plasters in my bag somewhere, just in case.

One of the nerdy joys of walking is the chance to buy all sorts of hi-tech and brightly coloured clothing to keep out the elements. So, don't leave any of it at home. In the picture on the left I had left my jacket at home and had to wear a plastic waterproof that was very hot and sweaty. I had also left my over trousers at home, so when the rain came my clothes gradually soaked up the water running off my jacket and channelled it round my back and legs in a cold and clammy flow.

The contrast when walking in driving rain with good waterproof jacket and functional

JW on Great Whernside
trying to look jolly while cold and wet.

over-trousers is incredible. Suddenly you are transformed and feel immune from discomfort and yet you are part of the storm; rain and wind becomes something to be enjoyed, welcomed, loved....

Before setting out on this walk make sure your over trousers, jacket and hat are still rain proof. New over trousers only cost £25 so, if in doubt, it would be a good idea to buy some.

Socks - everyone has their own solutions for comfortable feet, I like the double layered socks next to the skin, and the thick, spongy outer socks over the top. These are not the old fashioned 100% wool but the wool and wickable fibre mix, and did I say spongy? It is worth buying a new outer pair for each day of the walk. Socks with a nice cushion of material to protect your feet. Then if the soles of your feet feel hot, dunk them in the nearest stream and put on new socks for the rest of the day. At lunch-breaks take your boots off and spend the hour wiggling your toes under the table.

Which brings us to LUNCH. The most important essential that you cannot pack is food. This is a week in which it is allowed to eat too much. You will not gain weight unless you think a diet of burgers etc., is a good thing. While doing something as good for you as walking a hundred miles it is also a good thing to eat well, and eat often. For breakfast, why not try porridge, scrambled eggs on toast, more toast & marmalade? For lunch, reward yourself with a light tasty meal, something to look forward to as well as being very important. If you do not eat enough, by the third or fourth day it will suddenly be hard to get going. A sure sign is if your mood changes, you lose enthusiasm for an activity that you normally love. The human body finds it very difficult to run on empty. It shuts down to save what little energy is available, and that includes the brain, which uses a lot of energy, especially when it is required to motivate you to make the effort for the day ahead. There is a lunch time stop available on every day except one, and it is essential that you take advantage of them. Have a good curry (vegetarian), or pasta, something light and nutritious, something that isn't dead. The evening meal is another reward, and although you are not likely to have any difficulty getting to sleep after a full day's walk, good food will also make the night's sleep all the more restful. Don't forget a little glass of beer or wine with your meals.......

Before setting out please visit the website at www.bay2bay.co.uk where I will post up-to-date information as well as feedback from other walkers. You can send your experiences & photographs of either walk, East or West, so I can show what the walks are like for the real walkers.
Any problems you can email me at johnwhite@bay2bay.co.uk and I'll do my best to help.

And that is it. You are now prepared, so walk this way please ....West.

Day One
Terrain: Fields, hill tops and open moor
Distance: 15 miles
(8½ to Malham then 6½ to Settle)
Height Gain: 2800 feet
Maximum Height: (starting height 650 ft) 1750 ft
Constant walking time: 6 hours
Allow: 8 hours
Refreshments: Lots of options in Malham

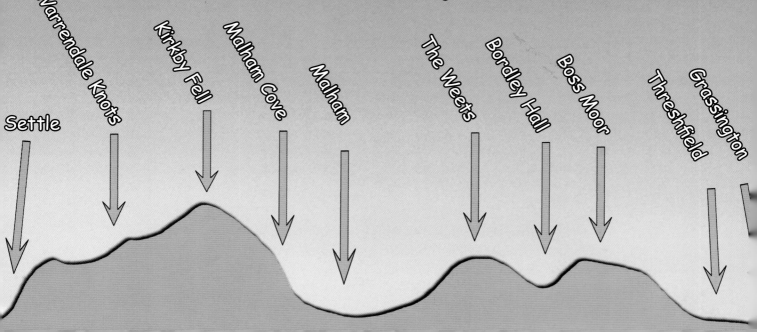

Settle · Warrendale Knots · Kirkby Fell · Malham Cove · Malham · The Weets · Bordley Hall · Boss Moor · Threshfield · Grassington

Day One.
Grassington to Settle via Malham

Walking west, towards the setting sun, on another adventure from the centre of the Dales. There is a steady start to the walk, not too dramatic, unless the weather is your friend and blows a lovely gale in from the West. What joy to be on the slopes of Boss Moor in a fierce westerly. Once you have gained a little height the view opens up to the south. Look out for Winterburn reservoir when you arrive at the top of the moor. The much bigger view south is one that stays with us for the next three or four days - Pendle Hill becomes a familiar landmark.

Although described as a lunchtime stop, Malham could just as easily be a good place to spend your first night, especially if you are not in a rush or want to walk yourself in.

Beyond Malham, there is a steady climb up the steps next to Malham Cove, this gets most of the climbing out of the way, and then into some fine high country across the moor to Warrendale Knots. If you like a bit of an adventure there is Horseshoe Cave and the lofty entrance to Attermire Cave to visit. Take a torch and potter up the steep slope to Attermire, find the wide ledge on the left of the cave entrance and then simply walk round to gain access to the cave. You can walk quite a long way in without a torch, round two corners so that you are in complete darkness (listen for the monster from the deep!). The joy of 'caves for kids', as Wainwright called them, is that they can be visited without ropes, snorkels and back up from the cave rescue services (or post traumatic counselling). Another advantage of this sort of cave is that the day looks so much brighter, when you come back out, whatever the weather!

Day 1. Grassington to Settle

WP01
Grassington
Square
1 mile
W to WP02

With the Devonshire Hotel on your right, the first steps of this walk lead down the square. At the

Grassington

bottom turn right down the road to Grassington Bridge and across the River Wharfe. Follow the road through Threshfield to the t-junction, turn left. **Map 1, p.12.**

WP02
0.9 miles
W to WP03

Turn right up the track beside the Old Hall Inn (see photo page 13) to find the first of 14 fine stiles in the corner under a tree. The stiles are all concentrated into a single mile. Most are nice stone stiles that

have been well maintained. At Grysedale Lane turn right and then first left onto a track to find a stile on the right. Two more fields brings you out onto the top end of Skirethorns Lane, turn left. **Map 2, p.13.**

Map 1. Grassington to Threshfield

12

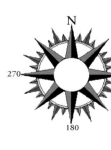

Map 2. Threshfield field paths with stile numbers

WP03
1.25 miles
W to WP04

Follow the walled track past a left hand fork, to a half right bend, beyond Lane House. Turn left through the wall and keep to the path uphill for the first field and then into the access land of Boss Moor. ...ntinue to the wall that runs along the rounded ridge top. Map 3, p.15.

Path next to the Old Hall Threshfield

WP04
0.4 miles
NW to WP05

Turn right through the gate into the walled lane, once again ignore the lane on the left but continue to just before the next right hand bend where there are gates on the right and left. Map 3, p.15.

Looking back towards Grassington

WP05
0.5 miles
NW to WP06

Take the left turn, across the field to a stile and gate in the wall ahead. Tend to the right and then follow the next wall down to join a track with Bordley Hall Farm clearly visible down below. Map 3, p.15/14.

WP06
0.6 miles
W to WP07

The path joins a wide track, turn left and then right onto tarmac and to continue downhill to Bordley Hall farm. The track circles round the back of the buildings to a gate. Go through and turn left, south, beginning to climb back up the other side of the valley. Near the first bend there is a path on the right heading west, away from the large track. Turn up it, right. Map 3, p.14.

WP07
0.5 miles
SW to WP08

Walk up the hill to the small paddock in front of a barn on the right, and then into a field beyond. Another building is over the wall on the right and Park House ahead. Map 4, p.17.

WP08
1 mile
W to WP09

Continue through the paddock behind Park House and then turn right to find the gate out into the field beyond. Through two fields with the wind-stunted trees and the wall on the right, cross a wall into a walled lane at a corner. Turn left to visit The Weets Top, a trig point and remains of a cross. Look over the wall on the right to see the famous terrain that indicates that Malham is close. Return down the lane to the corner and turn left, to arrive at a road at the bottom. Turn left. Map 4, p.17/16.

WP09
0.8 miles
W to WP10

Follow the road downhill, taking note of the change in the landscape. You are now crossing the Craven Fault, so the land west is dramatically different. At the bottom of the hill you should take another quick detour up the path to the right to see Gordale Scar. Walk up the ravine (only $\frac{1}{4}$ mile) until you are round the corner and can see the waterfall. If you are feeling energetic try climbing the big stone in the middle (it has enormous steps worn into it), then return to WP10. Map 4, p.16.

15

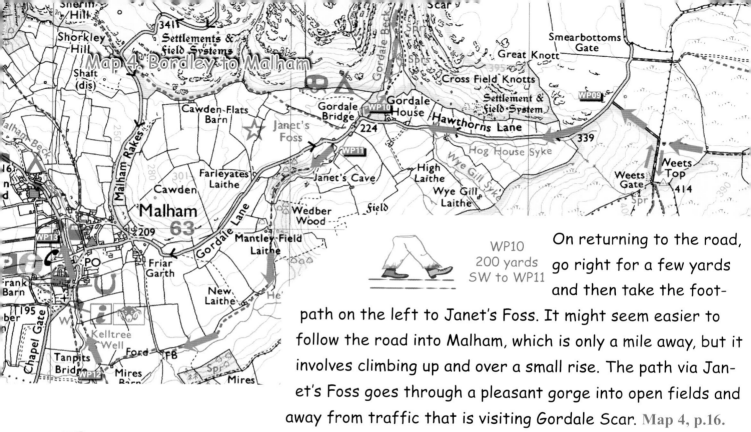

Map 4: Bordley to Malham

WP10
200 yards
SW to WP11

On returning to the road, go right for a few yards and then take the foot-path on the left to Janet's Foss. It might seem easier to follow the road into Malham, which is only a mile away, but it involves climbing up and over a small rise. The path via Janet's Foss goes through a pleasant gorge into open fields and away from traffic that is visiting Gordale Scar. **Map 4, p.16.**

WP11
1 mile
SW to WP12

Follow the obvious path out of the valley that contains Janet's Foss, out of the trees and across the fields. Keep going to the sharp bend and turn north to find the stream on your left. **Map 4, p.16.**

WP12
0.4 miles
N to WP13

Turn right and, with the stream on your left, walk to the village of Malham which is visible ahead. Time for LUNCH! **Map 4, p.16.**

Follow the road north out of Malham towards the famous Malham Cove. There is a farm on the right which helps direct you to the well marked path a few yards further up the road. Map 5, p.19.

WP13
0.25 miles
N to WP14

There is a clear path up the valley to the front of the Cove. It is only when you are near that you can see its real size. Map 5, p.19.

WP14
0.5 miles
N to WP15

Now for a work out! Turn left and enjoy a lovely climb up many, many steps to the top of the Cove. This climb is most of the remaining height gain for the rest of the day, so you might as well get it over with. Map 5, p.19.

WP15
0.2 miles
NW to WP16

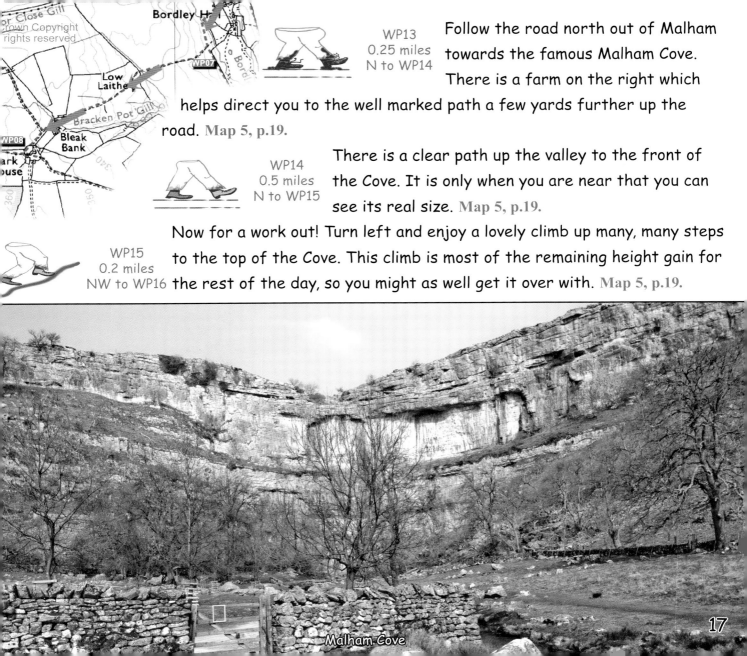

Malham Cove

17

Map 5. Malham to Settle

WP16
0.2 miles
N to WP17

At the top it might be a good idea to walk onto the limestone pavement that makes up the top of the Cove. Then follow the path north across the field until you get to a stile with a National Trust sign. Map 5, p.19.

WP17
500 yards
W to WP18

Cross the stile and turn sharp left along the edge of the wall to exit from the field into the road via a gate. Map 5, p.19. Go left back down the road towards Malham where a fingerpost in the corner points right. Map 5, p.19.

WP18
0.2 miles
S to WP19

WP19
2.7 miles
W to WP20

Follow the path that is on the other side of the gate. There are now nearly three miles

18

Lovely Steps and plenty of them

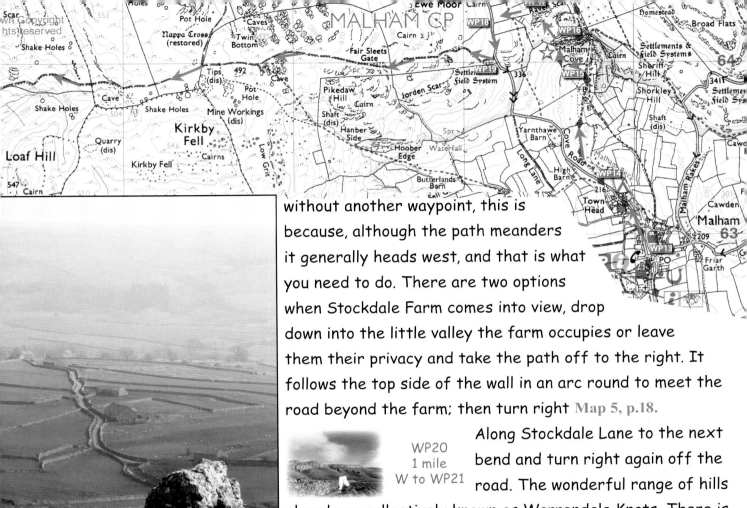

The view back towards Malham

without another waypoint, this is because, although the path meanders it generally heads west, and that is what you need to do. There are two options when Stockdale Farm comes into view, drop down into the little valley the farm occupies or leave them their privacy and take the path off to the right. It follows the top side of the wall in an arc round to meet the road beyond the farm; then turn right **Map 5, p.18.**

WP20
1 mile
W to WP21

Along Stockdale Lane to the next bend and turn right again off the road. The wonderful range of hills ahead are collectively known as Warrendale Knots. There is Horseshoe Cave up to the right and further on Attermire Cave. (If you climb the escarpment to Attermire you can walk along a grassy shelf and then stride round into the cave.) **Map 5, p.18.**

19

WP21
1.1 miles
W to WP22

The path climbs up the grassy slope west and then drops down quickly on the other side - Settle is visible below. Map 5, p.18.

WP22
0.4 miles
SW to WP23

The path turns left and follows the track down to a walled lane into the back streets of Settle. Follow the road downhill to emerge in the market place. Map 5, p.18.

Warrendale Knots

West Coast 85

Grassington 15

Day Two
Terrain: Foot hills and Ingleborough Hill
Distance: 15 miles
(7 miles to Clapham then 8 miles to Ingleton)
Height Gain: 3050 feet
Maximum Height: (starting from 500 ft) 2365 feet
Constant walking time: 6 hours
Refreshments: Pubs & Cafes at Feizor, Austwick, Clapham, Victoria Cave

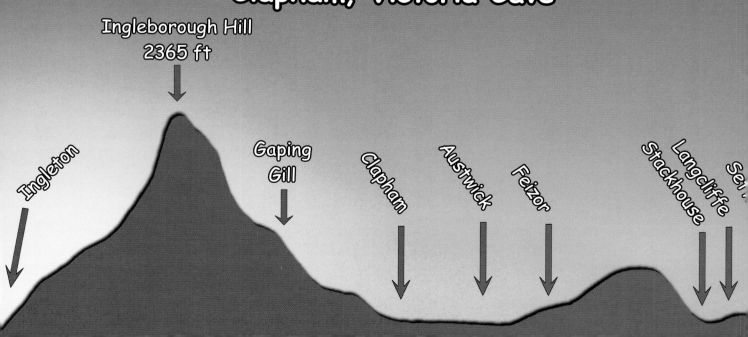

Ingleborough Hill
2365 ft

Ingleton

Gaping Gill

Clapham

Austwick

Feizor

Stackhouse

Langcliffe

Se...

Day Two.
Settle to Ingleton via Ingleborough Hill

Today involves a climb to the highest point of the whole walk, and the greatest combined height gain, so set out at a steady pace so that you arrive in Ingleton with enough enthusiasm left for tomorrow,.... and the next day!

It all starts easily enough, tootle up to Langcliffe, turn and head over to Feizor, followed by Austwick and eventually Clapham for lunch. If you are still taking your time, it could be a good idea to have another extra night at Clapham, which is set out here as a lunch time stop.

The way up Ingleborough is quite a long route so it is steady and probably the easiest. Trow Gill is such a wonderful fissure that it leads you up onto the flat land below the main climb onto Ingleborough without a great deal of effort. On the way you can have a look in Victoria Cave or just have a break for a cup of tea at the little cafe at its entrance.

If that westerly gale is still with you, the top of Ingleborough will be just the place to stop, have a sandwich, huddled down, ...fly a kite!

Day 2. Settle to Ingleton

WP01
1 mile
N to WP02

Walk back up towards Constitution Hill, to the left of the fine building in the small photograph on the page opposite. When you find the track you came down yesterday, continue instead along the tarmac, a back lane north towards Langcliffe. When the back road joins the main road up Ribblesdale, there are a couple of hundred yards to cover before you get to the houses at Langcliffe. Find the first ginnel on the left hand side of the road and turn down it towards the Langcliffe Mill buildings below. **Map 6, p.25.**

WP02
0.6 miles
NW to WP03

Follow the lovely ginnel down to the mill pond and buildings, turning right round the other side of the water, beyond which is a small footbridge across the river onto a track up to Stackhouse. **Map 6, p.25.**

WP03
0.3 miles
NW to WP04

Walk up the track and across the road, continuing straight on to find some strange canyon-like corners where the walls are high and imposing. Round the corner is a five bar gate with stone stile set into the wall. Head up the field to the three way fingerpost. **Map 6, p.25.**

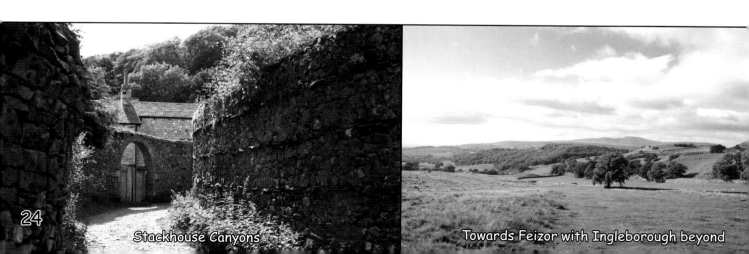

Stackhouse Canyons

Towards Feizor with Ingleborough beyond

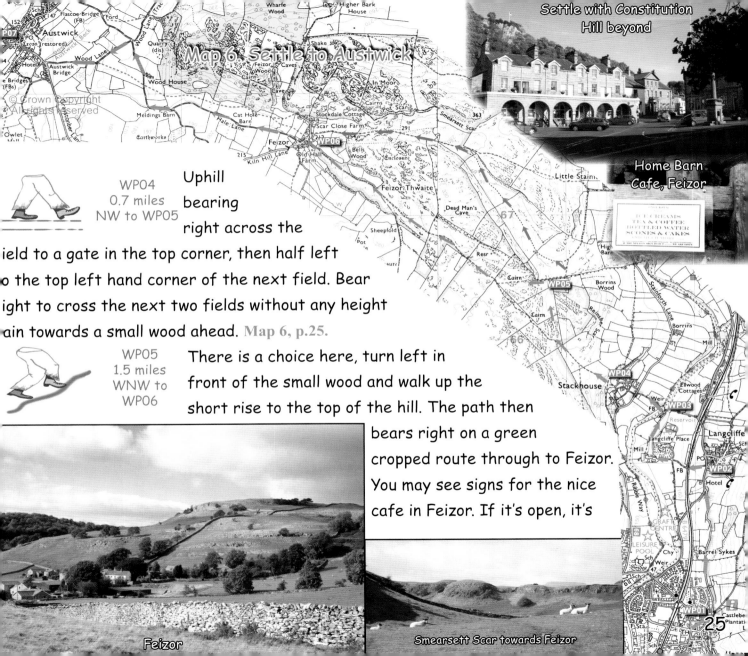

Map 6. Settle to Austwick

Settle with Constitution Hill beyond

Home Barn Cafe, Feizor

WP04
0.7 miles
NW to WP05

Uphill bearing right across the field to a gate in the top corner, then half left to the top left hand corner of the next field. Bear right to cross the next two fields without any height gain towards a small wood ahead. **Map 6, p.25.**

WP05
1.5 miles
WNW to WP06

There is a choice here, turn left in front of the small wood and walk up the short rise to the top of the hill. The path then bears right on a green cropped route through to Feizor. You may see signs for the nice cafe in Feizor. If it's open, it's

Feizor

Smearsett Scar towards Feizor

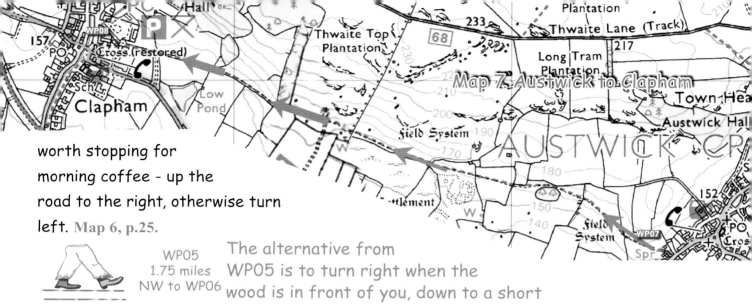

worth stopping for
morning coffee - up the
road to the right, otherwise turn
left. **Map 6, p.25.**

WP05
1.75 miles
NW to WP06

The alternative from WP05 is to turn right when the wood is in front of you, down to a short walled lane and then left into the field. Bear left to follow the path up the middle of the fantastic valley with, after a couple of fields, Smearsett Scar and Pot Scar up ahead on the right. The path then bears left downhill into Feizor. Turn left to find the next path towards Austwick. **Map 6, p.25.**

WP06
1.6 miles
W to WP07

The best path to Austwick is Hale Lane a short way along the road on the right by a big barn. This is a fine walled lane that sweeps you along with the greatest of ease. Even when the track meets another at Meldings Barn, the route is clear and clearly marked. You can follow this into Austwick, or when the field path crosses the walled track, (two ladder stiles opposite each other) turn left through one field to cut off a couple of corners. But the walled lane is so good, it is probably difficult to leave it. From Wood Lane turn left into Austwick. **Map 6, p.25.**

Approaching Ingleborough Cave

WP07
1.6 miles
NW to WP08

There is a nice pub in Austwick, The Game Cock, but with another twelve miles to walk today it is probably better to take lunch at Clapham, only 1½ miles further across the fields. Access the field path by a stone stile on the right a few hundred yards down the road (left) from the pub. The path follows the flat remains of lynchets, the old fields that have terraced many of the hillsides across the Dales. At the end of the third field, there is a stile in the wall in front, but the path continues round the corner of the wall down to the left where there is another stile. The rest of the path is easily followed all the way to Clapham. **Map 7 p.26.**

WP08
0.25 miles
N to WP09

The New Inn - is just around to the left. It is a hotel, so if you are planning to have a shorter day it might be a good place to stay. At least have a hearty lunch in preparation for the steady climb ahead. After lunch, whether at the pub or one of several good cafes, walk through the village to the church at the top. **Map 8 p.27.**

Map 8.
Clapham to
Ingleborough

The top of Trow Gill

WP09
1.3 miles
N to WP10

At the church turn up to the left, sign posted for the Ingleborough Cave and trail. This is through a farm yard just round the corner. There is a 'pay & display' type of meter for a 50 pence ticket to walk through the estate. It is worth this sma fee because the path is beside the lake and through pleasant trees and next to a gorge. If you cannot afford the fee continue past the farm gate and you will see a fingerpost pointing right. Follow this to Clapdale Farm and then turn right again to rejoin the Clapdale path which leads up Trow Gill. Eventually you arrive at Ingleborough Cave, a brilliant show cave with a small hut at the entrance that serves tea, coffee and biscuits. **Map 8 p.27.**

WP10
0.6 miles
N to WP11

The rest of Trow Gill gradually becomes more rugged until it narrows to a rocky scramble out on to the moor **Map 8 p.27.**

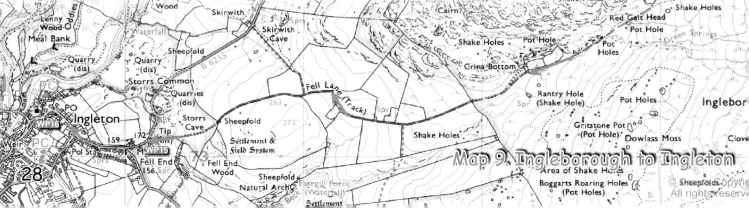
Map 9. Ingleborough to Ingleton

Looking towards Little Ingleborough

WP11
0.7 miles
NW to WP12

Cross the first stretch of moor to the fenced off and scary maw that is the top of Gaping Gill pot. It boasts a cavern floor 300ft directly below this innocuous looking hole in the ground Map 8 p.27.

WP12
0.8 miles
NW to WP13

The way is along an obvious path up Little Ingleborough, to the southern shoulder of the hill. Map 8 p.27.

When you get to Little Ingleborough it still looks quite a distance to the top but it is less than a mile.

WP13
0.9 miles
N to WP14

Keep going, most of this day has been uphill but from the top it is downhill all the way. Map 8 p.27.

On most days, with a bit of luck, the weather will be clear enough to see Morecambe Bay from here. There is a brass pointer set into the three walled wind break

WP14
3 miles
SW to WP15

that is on the top. Turn south west to find the wide and obvious path all the way down to Ingleton. The path leaves the open moor into a shallow valley known as Crina Bottoms, and at the end joins a walled lane that leads to the road at Ingleton. Map 9 p.28.

WP15
0.5 miles
SW to WP16

Cross the road to find the centre of the village a short stroll downhill. Map 9 p.28.

West Coast 70

Grassington 30

Day Three
Terrain: Steady climb open moor
Distance: 16 miles
(12½ miles to Barbon then 3½ to Kirkby Lonsdale)
Alternative ridge walk: +1 mile
Constant walking time: 8 hours
Total Height gain: 2800 feet
Highest point: (starting from 200 ft) 2050 feet
Refreshment: None until Barbon
Take two packed lunches

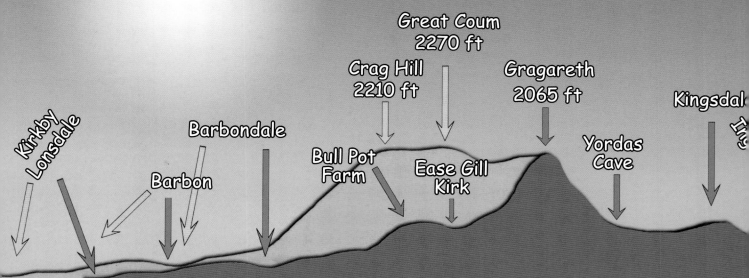

Kirkby Lonsdale

Barbondale

Barbon

Great Coum
2270 ft

Crag Hill
2210 ft

Gragareth
2065 ft

Kingsdal

Bull Pot
Farm

Ease Gill
Kirk

Yordas
Cave

Day Three.
Ingleton to Kirkby Lonsdale

After the lofty heights of yesterday, today is a journey into the wild. There is a cave to explore, so remember to take a torch, it is a nice safe cave, dark, dripping and slightly muddy underfoot, but safe, well almost safe. It is also a day without the chance of a lunch time stop, or for that matter, the opportunity to break this quite long day into two. There is a fine pub at Barbon, which is well on through the day, but it provides an option for a well earned pint.

So take two packed lunches, one for necessity and the second for comfort. You will also climb the steepest, although not the highest, hill on the walk - Gragareth. At the top there are two options, the favoured route is a high level walk along the ridge north following the top of Gragareth to Great Coum and then down the end of Crag Hill into Barbon Dale. It is favoured, but in poor weather it may not worth the effort. The shorter route (one mile shorter and somewhat easier terrain) is straight off the top of Gragareth into Ease Gill, where you should visit Ease Gill Kirk, a dry waterfall in the river bed. The terrain for both routes then changes from quite hard going to extremely easy and pastoral. So a great mix of waterfalls, gorges, caves, steep slopes, long ridges, hidden features and vast open spaces. All you need is a blustery squall to complete a perfect day.

Looking up Kingsdale

Day 3. Ingleton to Kirkby Lonsdale

WP01
0.2 miles
W to WP02

Walk west across the bridge in Ingleton to the entrance to Ingleton Glen Walk. It costs £3.50 to walk up past the waterfalls. Well worth it too. **Map 10, p.34**.

WP02
1.8 miles
N to WP03

Follow the obvious path past the brilliant waterfalls in the Glen to Ravenray Footbridge at the top. Cross the bridge and walk up the slope to the walled lane. Map 10, p.34.

WP03
1.7 miles
N to WP04

Turn right to find a gate that gives access to the field and the path north up the right hand side of Kingsdale (photo page 32). This is access land so you do not need to find the beginning of the path, which once you are in the field is up to the right. This path is easily followed to Braida Garth Farm visible in the distance. The route through the farm is not clear. Walk to the middle of the buildings and turn left

33

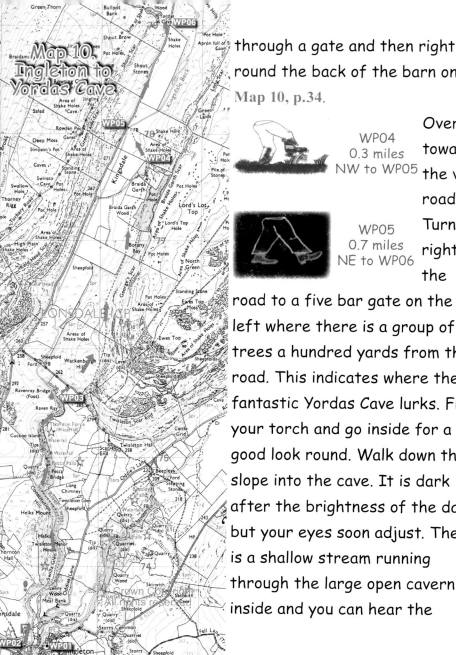

Map 10.
Ingleton to
Yordas Cave

through a gate and then right up the grass bank and right again round the back of the barn on the right. The stile is in the wall ahead. Map 10, p.34.

WP04
0.3 miles
NW to WP05

Over the stile turn half left across the field towards the footbridge at the bottom of the valley, where the stream is close to the road. Map 10, p.34.

WP05
0.7 miles
NE to WP06

Turn right up the road to a five bar gate on the left where there is a group of trees a hundred yards from the road. This indicates where the fantastic Yordas Cave lurks. Find your torch and go inside for a good look round. Walk down the slope into the cave. It is dark after the brightness of the day, but your eyes soon adjust. There is a shallow stream running through the large open cavern inside and you can hear the

Stone on Twistleton Scar

ashing of water as though you are going to get really wet, do not be put off. The noise is a waterfall fifty yards up to right, in the corner behind a screen of rock. Map 10, p.34.

WP06
1.2 miles
W to WP07

After a pleasant splash round inside the cave, emerge, glad to be alive, into the sunshine once again. Have r first lunch here if you haven't already had it! The choice routes start from here. See the section at the end of this pter for the highly recommended Gragareth Ridge walk. On t route you begin by walking North West to the top of agareth, but miss visiting the trig point. On the standard te turn up the slopes behind the cave, heading for the mit and trig point of Gragareth, which is very slightly th of the cave. Both routes offers the steepest climb on e whole walk, although not the highest. Map 11, p.37.

WP07
0.9 miles
SW to WP08

When you are at the trig point walk west, downhill passing the three cairns called the Three Men of agareth. When you arrive at a track turn left towards Leck ll House, it is the only house up this side of the valley, The lds around it are not part of access land so please respect eir privacy. Walk to the wall past the house to where the

Exit from Yordas Cave

Yordas Cave
hidden waterfall

You have followed this wall from Leck Fell House

Follow this wall to Bull Pot Farm

Ease Gill Kirk is down in these trees

Ease Gill Moor

track becomes tarmac and turn right into the first field that is access land. Map 11, p.37.

WP08
1.1 miles
NW to WP09

Follow the wall on your right until you drop down into Ease Gill, a dry stream bed. Ease Gill Kirk is downstream to the left, keep to the bank on the far side and follow a little path until you can walk round the end of some rocks to find the hidden mystery of the ancient dry waterfall and collapsed cave. Map 11, p.37.

WP09
0.8 miles
N to WP10

This is a good place for a second lunch. Climb out of the gully, until you can see a derelict building on the other side of the wall. Do not cross the wall but follow it north to Bull Pot Farm. Map 11, p.37.

WP10
1.1 miles
N to WP11

Bull Pot Farm is a potholers re-source, so there are often cars and people dressed in rubber and fes-tooned with painful looking equipment pottering about..... Turn left across the front of the buildings and then right onto the grassy track. The track becomes a sheep trod across the

Ease Gill Kirk

Map 11. Yordas to Barbondale
& The Great Coum Ridge Walk

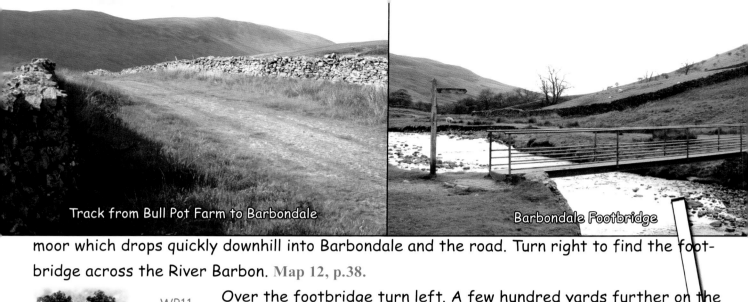

Track from Bull Pot Farm to Barbondale

Barbondale Footbridge

moor which drops quickly downhill into Barbondale and the road. Turn right to find the foot-bridge across the River Barbon. Map 12, p.38.

WP11
1.6 miles
W to WP12

Over the footbridge turn left. A few hundred yards further on the path enters pleasant woodland, with the river on your left. This woodland walk is a striking contrast to the emptiness of the land you have recently crossed. The path is like a walk through the woods of a stately home - probably Barbon Manor, which can be glimpsed through the trees. Leave the wood at Pencil Brow to join a small tarmac road that winds across the field. Map 12, p.38.

Map 12. Barbondale

WP12
0.2 miles
S to WP13

The road curves round the edge of the field towards the pretty church in the village. If you want some good food and beer the Barbon Inn is just along the road to the right. Otherwise cross the road through a stile onto a path in the field. **Map 12, p.38.**

Barbon Woods

WP13
0.4 miles
S to WP14

Cross the middle of the field up a slight rise. At the far hedge climb into a walled track. Turn left and in a few yards leave the track into another field and cross hat to the house at Underfell. At the road turn right downhill for 200 yards and then left gain through a gap stile. **Map 13, p.40.**

WP14
0.9 miles
S to WP15

Follow the right hand edge of the fields towards Low Bank House. Then the path bends left and joins a gravel road, keep left, away from the farm and follow the fence on your right round the right hand cor-

Barbon village

ner, to find a stile into the field ahead. Cross the dip that runs through the field and climb onto higher ground but keep to the middle of the field to Whelprigg. Cross the land in front of Whelprigg House, it is visible up to the left (photo page 41). You cross the driveway and the stile beyond is at the fence ahead. Cross four more fields south to the road at Fell Garth. Map 13, p.40.

WP15
0.3 miles
SE to WP16

Go straight on, across the road, following the fingerpost down the left hand side of the house and across the end of their garden for only twenty yards to a stile in the corner into a field. Go up the field to the gate. Turn half right through another gate to follow a path towards the house with tennis courts that can be seen ahead. The path looks as though it is going into the

Casterton
Church

40

grounds of the house but there is a stile in the wall on the left just before you get there. Walk along the edge of the field and then left up a slight rise to keep with the right hand field boundary. Through a gate and on until you climb a ladder stile into a lane with a house down to the right. Map 13, p.40.

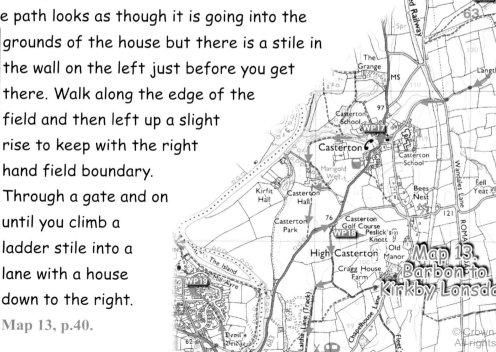

Whelprigg Estate

WP16
0.7 miles
W to WP17

Turn right to follow a tarmac track that leads towards Casterton. Straight on at the cross road, then under the railway bridge to arrive at Casterton with the church on your right. There is a ginnel down the right side of the church which leads to the main road. Map 13, p.40.

WP17
0.8 miles
W & S
to WP18

Cross this road and follow the track bearing left onto a gravel road and past a house with nicely clipped bushes. In a wood, there is a five bar gate on the right with a yellow arrow on it which is not the way to go. Continue to the next gate which is on the left (into a house driveway) and the path bends to the right. At the kissing-

Path through Casterton

gate ahead there is a sign for Kirkby Lonsdale, turn left into the field and follow the diversion round Casterton Hall. It goes up to the left and along the driveway to a well signed fingerpost, (there is a little short cut from here if you look at the map). Otherwise, turn right down the hill almost to the hall again, where the path turns left into the field. Follow this to the road and turn left as far as the golf club where a ginnel leads off to the right. Map 13, p.40.

WP18
1.3 miles
S&W
to WP19

This path follows the edge of the golf course and then after quarter of a mile takes a right turn and a left bend which runs alongside a

caravan park. It emerges at the end of a caravan park near to Kirkby Lonsdale, turn right and walk along the road to cross Devil's Bridge. On the other side of the bridge the riverside path takes you up stream, it is a little further but a very pleasant circuit round to the centre of Kirkby without any problem. Or a couple of hundred yards further on there is a right turn up a ginnel that brings you to the Kirkby Lonsdale square. Map 13, p.40.

Kirkby Lonsdale

Gragareth Ridge

Alternative Route: Gragareth Ridge to Barbondale via Great Coum (6 miles)

This route only adds about one mile to the day's efforts, which means you will have walked about $17\frac{1}{2}$ miles by the time you get to Kirkby Lonsdale. On a bright day, in either winter or summer, it will be an absolute joy. On a wet day it could be a little more difficult and less rewarding. The compelling reason for doing this route is to be able to see the views in all directions. The usual experience with hill walking is that you spend an hour or two climbing a hill, have a sandwich and drink on the top for twenty minutes and then head down the other side. With this route you get to spend a couple of hours enjoying the height you have put so much effort into gaining. The walk passes the County

Stone, where Yorkshire, Lancashire and the old county of Westmorland once met. The ridge itself is grass covered for most of the way. When one side of the wall is a bit boggy, the other side is often quite dry. Changing from one side of the wall to the other also crosses between Yorkshire and Lancashire, so you can quickly see if it rains more in one or the other! The harder part of the alternative route is the path-less descent into Barbondale, which is two miles of tussock grass and steady downhill walking. If it is wet and the views obscured, it could be quite hard work.

WP01
1.1 miles
NW to WP02

If you have committed to this alternative route, do not climb towards the trig point on Gragareth from Yordas Cave, instead go straight up to the top or take a diagonal route north west across the hillside to join the ridge. Map 11, p.37.

WP02
2.1 miles
N to WP03

When you make it to the ridge turn right, due north, and follow the ridge wall. After about one and a half miles look for a wall on the left that joins the ridge wall. In the crook of the join sits the County Stone. Hopefully, you will have a clear day and stunning panoramic views. The Lake District. Dent Dale to the north and Howgill Fells beyond. Ingleborough back east. This is an amazing fell top. Map 11, p.37.

WP03
0.6 miles
W to WP04

At Great Coum turn left and follow the ridge to Crag Hill, only half a mile west. Map 11, p.37.

WP04
2.4 miles
W to WP05

This is access land, so there are no paths. From Crag Hill trig point head West until you reach the road through Barbondale. Note that not all the land is open access and respect the privacy of several fields that surround Fell House just before you get to the road.

At the road turn left until you can rejoin the main route at the footbridge across the River Barbon at WP11. Map 11, p.37.

West Coast 54

Grassington 46

Miles of Wonderful Walls

DAY FOUR
Terrain: Climb to Newbiggin Crags
Distance: 14 miles
(8 miles to Burton-in-Kendal then 6 miles to Silverdale)
Constant walking time: 5 hours
Total Height gain: 1350 feet
Highest Point: (starting from 220 ft) 800 feet
Refreshment: Burton-in-Kendal

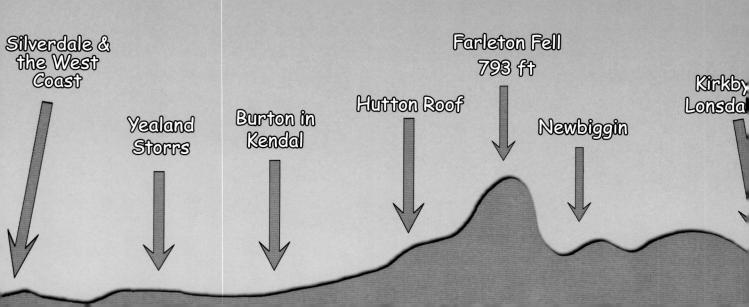

Silverdale & the West Coast

Yealand Storrs

Burton in Kendal

Hutton Roof

Farleton Fell
793 ft

Newbiggin

Kirkby Lonsdale

Day Four.
Kirkby Lonsdale to Silverdale

This is the day you arrive at the coast. The land you have crossed has been fairly challenging, even in good weather, more so in rain, and probably quite hard going if you have walked into the teeth of that westerly gale I keep invoking for your pleasure. Don't thank me yet....

Now, apart from the great sense of achievement and the wonderful country that you have crossed, you get a third reward on this day, easier walking, new and unheard of fells, fantastic views both forwards and back.

This day leaves the high hills to gradually settle down into some rolling hills and small craggy tops before arriving at the flat edge of the long coast. It is still a limestone day, heading for the stunning limestone pavements and natural sculptures of Newbiggin Crags.

Then, beyond Burton-in-Kendal the final few miles are characterised by the bird reserves around Leighton Moss. You do not have to visit Leighton Moss itself to get the feeling that birds and wildlife are comfortable in this corner of the country, their presence extends across the hills and dales to the coast. You walk past the little lake called Hawes Water, surrounded by reeds and filled with the song and twitter of bird life. Welcome to the West Coast....

Day 4. Kirkby Lonsdale to Silverdale

WP01
0.5 miles
SW to WP02

Head out of Kirkby Lonsdale along Biggins Road to the A65 road turn right and then cross and continue, left, to Low Biggins. Two hundred yards from the main road, on the right, there is a metal kissing gate into the field. Map 14, p.49.

WP02
0.5 miles
W to WP03

Cross the field and then into the pleasant wood that leads through to High Biggins. At the road continue straight on. A quarter of a mile later there is a track on the left and in the corner of the hedge a gap stile into the field, (Pit Lane turn photo, below). Map 14, p.49.

WP03
1 mile
NW to WP04

Walk across the field to another stile that leads into a short fenced-in path next to holding pens, at the end of this path cross another stile into the field, turn right. The path keeps high in this field but tends slowly away from the top wall to a stile in the wall about 200 yards ahead. Cross the next two fields, tending in the same direction, moving further away from the

Low Biggins to High Biggins path

Pit Lane turn

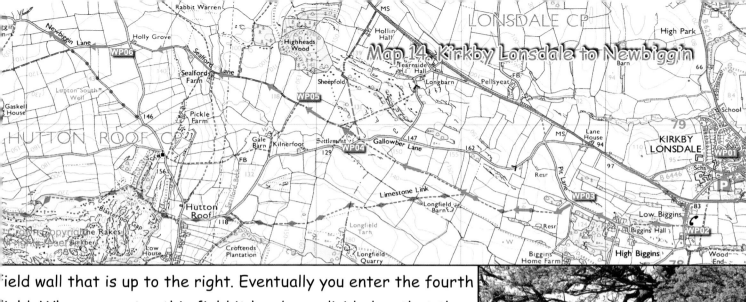

Map 14. Kirkby Lonsdale to Newbiggin

field wall that is up to the right. Eventually you enter the fourth field. When you enter this field it has been divided so that the top wall is now close on your right. The path follows this wall to the far corner where it divides, keep right and with the wall still on your right cross a further three fields to Gallowber Lane. **Map 14, p.49.**

WP04
0.3 miles
SW to WP05

Cross Gallowber Lane and continue across the next two fields until you find the hedged lane shown here. **Map 14, p.49.**

WP05
0.8 miles
W to WP06

Follow this wonderful ancient path until it becomes Sealford Lane and turns to tarmac next to Sealford Farm. Keep on to the cross roads at Holly Grove. **Map 14, p.49.**

Ancient path beyond
Gallowber Lane

49

Limestone Scars on Newbiggin Crags

View of Farleton Fell from Hutton Roof

WP06
1 mile
W to WP07

This is Newbiggin Lane which leads to the small hamlet of Newbiggin. When the road joins another from the left among the houses, go straight on. Map 15, p.51.

WP07
0.3 miles
S to WP08

After the last house on the left there is a path and fingerpost that gives access to the fell. The path turns back left to climb steadily up the hillside. Map 15, p.51.

WP08
1.5 miles
SW to WP09

From this point the route takes a quick circuit round the wonderful limestone landscape that covers the top of the fell. Head slightly north of west, only a short climb to the edge of a huge angled cap of limestone. It is dotted with a mixture of sculpted rocks and fine trees. It is well worth the short distance that is added to the walk to test your ankles in this unique terrain. Don't just walk straight through, zig-zag around and visit the boulders & trees that are dotted about. Eventually you should walk down the slope until you meet a path, part of the Limestone Link, and turn left to a gate in the wall. Map 15, p.51.

WP09
0.5 miles
S to WP10

Through the gate immediately leave the main path on a smaller path to the right. Head towards the small road between you and Hutton Roof. Turn right along the road for about three hundred yards to a gate and fingerpost on the left into a field (photo page 53). Map 15, p.51.

WP10
1.6 miles
SW to WP11

Cross the field and enter the woods. The path turns right with the lower slopes of Hutton Roof up to your left. Follow it to a corner and a gate where the path becomes Slape Lane, a walled lane that takes you through to the edge of Burton-in-Kendal. Turn right and then left onto the main road through Burton, and follow for about half a mile to find the King's Arms on the right. A good place for lunch. Map 15, p.50/51.

Limestone Sculptures on Newbiggin Crag

← Crossing M6 with Farleton Fell

Fierce Puss →

Tree on Newbiggin Crag

Turn towards Hutton Roof

WP11
1 mile
NW to WP12

The first task after lunch is find our way across the M6. Turn left, back up the main street to a turning on the left. A couple of hundred yards down this road you will see a road called Drover's Way that heads towards the M6 and is marked as a footpath but unfortunately is a dead end. Continue for another fifty yards to the next road and turn left. Cross the M6 in a few hundred yards and beyond that walk through the long tunnel under the canal. Keep on the road and pass under the railway bridge, then bear left and at the road on the left turn towards Hilderstone Farm. Before you get to the farm look for a path on the right and turn up there. Map 15, p.50.

WP12
0.8 miles
W to WP13

This track leads through to the busy A6. Cross the road to where there is a wide verge and after about a quarter of a mile look for a fingerpost, which is well hidden in the hedge. There is a diagonal path, across the field behind the farm, (the field had a small herd of horses wandering about, they persuaded me to go round!). The other way is along the road to turn right up the farm track. Map 16, p.54.

WP13
1.2 miles
W to WP14

Negotiate the farm yard (where a fierce kitten came at me from behind the shed) and cross the same field just at the left hand corner, in through the gate and out just twenty yards along the left hand hedge. Head towards the corner of the woods. Then keep to the lower edge of the wood to the next corner where a fingerpost points left over a rising field to the little village of Yealand Storrs. Turn right at the road and follow round to where the road forks. Ahead there is a gate into Yealand Hall Allotment and a clear path into the trees. Map 16, p.54.

WP14
1 mile
W to WP15

Stroll along until the path comes back to the edge of the wood near a field on the left with large stones in the middle, look for a stile on the left into the next open field. It crosses the middle of the field to the

54

right hand wall (see photo below), and then crosses that field to the far corner where it enters the woods near Hawes Water. **Map 16, p.54.**

WP15
0.5 miles
SW to WP16

Turn right for a few hundred yards, on duck boards close to the lake, and then to a gate that cuts across the top of the lake to the road near Challan Hall, turn left. (If the lake is full you may have to walk the extra 200 yards round the end). Challan Hall, on the left, is a B&B (see Accommodation list) which could be attractive for anyone who doesn't mind shortening this day's walk by a mile, and being at least a mile away from the attractions (pubs) of Silverdale. **Map 16, p.54.**

WP16
1.5 miles
SW to WP17

Walk along the road past Challan Hall, look for a path on the right which takes you over one field to another road, across which is a rail-way line. If you miss the path just turn right at the junction and find the path over the railway line a hundred yards up the road on the left. (The trains are quite regular so take care when you cross). This takes you through Waterslack Farm where you enter Eaves Wood, which is another wood round here that has fantastic paths. Walk for about half a mile to the left turn out of Eaves Wood at Elmslack, coming out on the road opposite the cemetery. Turn right and then take the first left to find the centre of Silverdale.

Map 16, p.54.

Towards Hawes Water woods

West Coast 40

Grassington 60

Eaves Wood

DAY FIVE
Terrain: Beach, two hills and train
Distance: (walking) 7½ miles
(4 miles to Arnside then 3½ miles (on the train) to Grange-over-Sands, followed by 3½ miles to Cartmel)
Constant walking time: 3 hours
Time on Train: 6 minutes!
Total Height gain: 1400 feet
Highest point: (starting from 100 ft) 720 feet
Refreshment: Arnside & Grange-over-Sands

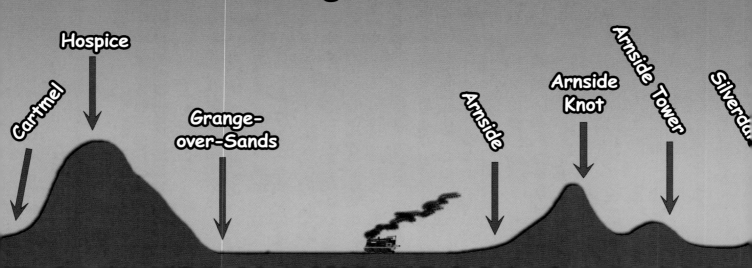

Cartmel
Hospice
Grange-over-Sands
Arnside
Arnside Knot
Arnside Tower
Silverda...

Day Five.
Silverdale to Cartmel

Have you noticed that this day only plans for seven or eight miles of walking? Eight miles is like a day off after the rigours of the last few days. So, buy a newspaper, plan for morning coffee in Arnside, lunch and afternoon tea in Grange-over-Sands and an early evening stroll round Cartmel before a good meal.

The day begins with a walk along the beach, followed by a visit to an ancient tower. Then, after 'nipping' up Arnside Knot, and jogging down the other side it will be time for coffee and cake in Arnside.

AFTER THAT WE CATCH THE TRAIN!

There are two reasons for this break with our boots, one is that the route round, although starting in very pleasant countryside, unfortunately soon requires a little stretch of quiet lane, followed by a little more of busier road, and then that becomes a very busy road across the bridge over the estuary. It is fourteen miles of unnecessary struggle rather than six minutes of calm.

If this day's walk is not really far enough for you, I have included accommodation at Haverthwaite, so you could do the first half of tomorrow's walk (6 miles). This would give you time to take a trip up Windermere on the Steam Railway and connecting boat, then when you come back a shorter walk between Haverthwaite and Ulverston (about 9 miles). This variation in overnight stops can be continued beyond Ulverston, by staying at Bardsea or Baycliff, making it possible to arrive at Rampside with time to visit Piel Island on the same day.

Day Five: Silverdale to Cartmel.

WP01
1 mile
N to WP02

We start with a walk down to the foreshore past the Silverdale Hotel. Walk along the stony beach itself round the first little headland of rocks to the next inlet. Turn right up the shingle to a gate onto a narrow road. Up the road to a junction (on a tight corner) turn left and follow the road to the next left hand bend. The entrance to a caravan park will be in front of you. Map 17, p.58.

WP02
0.7 miles
N to WP03

Walk through the caravan park, the path follows the contour, bearing right. In the middle of the park there is a clear signpost towards Arnside Tower which is further round the hill. Map 17, p.58.

WP03
0.5 miles
N to WP04

From the tower, walk left downhill through the farm and up to the road. At the road turn right for 500 yards where a fingerpost on the left points up into the trees. Map 17, p.58.

WP04
0.3 miles
NW to WP05

Bear left after you have gained some height to find the top of Arnside Knot. From the top of the Knot you can see Arnside below. Map 17, p.58.

Arnside Tower

WP05
1.4 miles
N to WP06

Head downhill and find the path through the trees and then the streets to the waters edge. There is a signpost for a path directly to the station if you do not intend to stop in Arnside. If you visit the town for morning coffee, follow the estuary wall round towards the viaduct and then a further 500 yards to Arnside Station to catch the next train to Grange-over-Sands. Map 17, p.58.

WP06
3.3 miles
W to WP07

Don't take a book to read as the journey only lasts six minutes. The line crosses the estuary to Grange-over-Sands with fine views of the sea or the sands. Map 18, p.61.

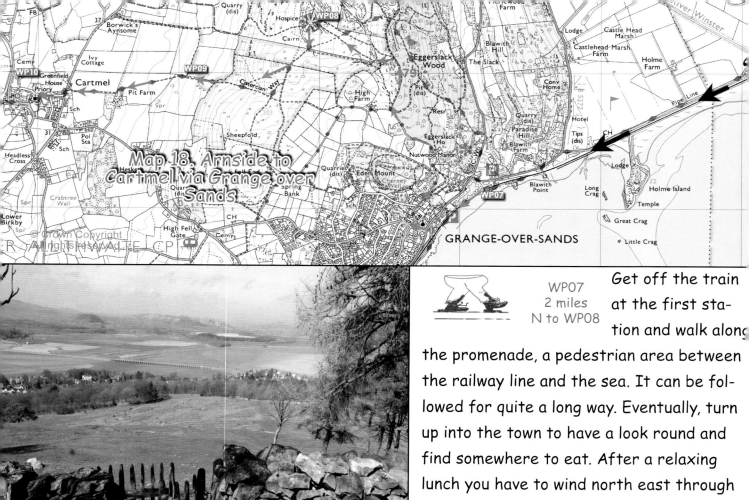

Map 18. Arnside to Cartmel via Grange over Sands

GRANGE-OVER-SANDS

Arnside from Arnside Knot.

WP07
2 miles
N to WP08

Get off the train at the first station and walk along the promenade, a pedestrian area between the railway line and the sea. It can be followed for quite a long way. Eventually, turn up into the town to have a look round and find somewhere to eat. After a relaxing lunch you have to wind north east through the streets for a short way to discover a track along the bottom edge of Eden Mount an attractive wooded hillside behind Grange. Do not go uphill into the wood. Continue to a point where there is an open field on the

Hospice

Built in 1846 by the vicar of Cartmel, this stone tower, known as the Hospice, was apparently built to provided shelter for travellers. Why they would walk up to the top of a hill when a park bench in Grange was likely to be more comfortable, I do not know. On a clear day you can see, with the help of a sighting device on the top, the Old Man of Coniston, Helvellyn, The Langdales and Morecambe Bay. I could also identify Piel Castle 15 miles away across the Leven Estuary.

Hospice

left and follow the wall round and uphill towards High Farm. Before the farm, turn right for a quarter of a mile and then through a gate, turn up the hillside sharp left to find the Hospice Tower. **Map 18, p.60.**

WP08
0.5 miles
SW WP09

Climb the precarious steps at the side of the tower to get a great view of the Lakeland Hills (and a useful pointer to identify them). Over to the west, on a clear day I could see the unmistakable silhouette of Piel Castle. Head south from the Tower on a well defined path which follows the ridge. The path drops off the ridge to the right, with Cartmel visible below. **Map 18, p.60.**

View of the Cumbrian Hills

WP09
1.1 miles
W to WP10

Go through the gate into a large field with Pit Farm at the far side. The path crosses the middle of the field directly towards the right hand edge of the farm. It skirts round the end of the barn and then turns to the left where there is a stile into the next field on the right. On the other side of the field the edge of Cartmel is reached down a dark hedged ginnel. Beyond, a few turns through the streets of Cartmel bring you to the square. **Map 18, p.60.**

West Coast 33

Grassington 67

Tree on Humphrey Head near Grange

Day Six

Terrain: High Coastal ridge, estuary paths
Distance: 14 miles
(6 miles to Haverthwaite then 8 miles to Ulverston)
Walking time: 5 hours
Total height gain: 1175 feet
Highest point: (starting from 90 ft) 590 feet
Refreshment: Pub or Cafe at Haverthwaite

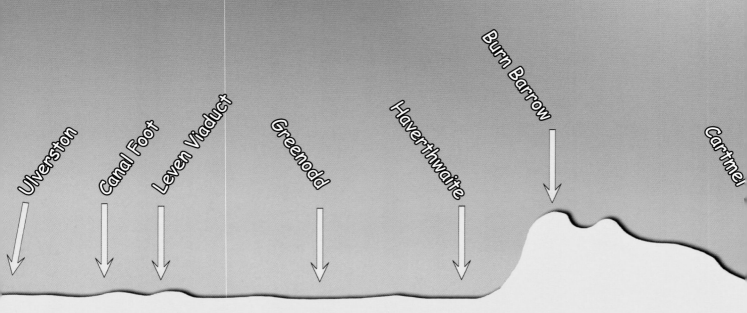

Day Six.
Cartmel to Ulverston

The change in the landscape today is subtle. It is not so much Pennine limestone, more Lake District limestone. There is also a widening of the horizon as you climb, and the enormous Morecambe Bay sky opens up.

Beyond Cartmel we climb onto the ridge nearby. Although the Cumbrian Coastal Path is heading in the same direction, I have chosen a different route that gives easier navigation and is away from fields full of grumpy looking cows. The idea is to keep out in the open where we can look at the sky and drift off into whatever thoughts accompany us when the pace is steady and uninterrupted by consultation of the map or this guide book.

If you really have a lot of time and can fit in an extra day, there is a fine excursion from Haverthwaite by steam train to Lakeside on Windermere. From here you can sail majestically up the lake to Bowness or Ambleside.

After Greenodd, the path follows the edge of the Leven Estuary, which is always an interesting place to be, whether the tide is in or out. This is definitely a walk to have a pair of binoculars with you. Ulverston is a nice little town, famous, among other things as the birthplace of Stan Laurel, so it is a good idea to take along a little bowler hat so that you fit in with all the locals who always wear one when they go out.....

Day 6. Cartmel to Ulverston

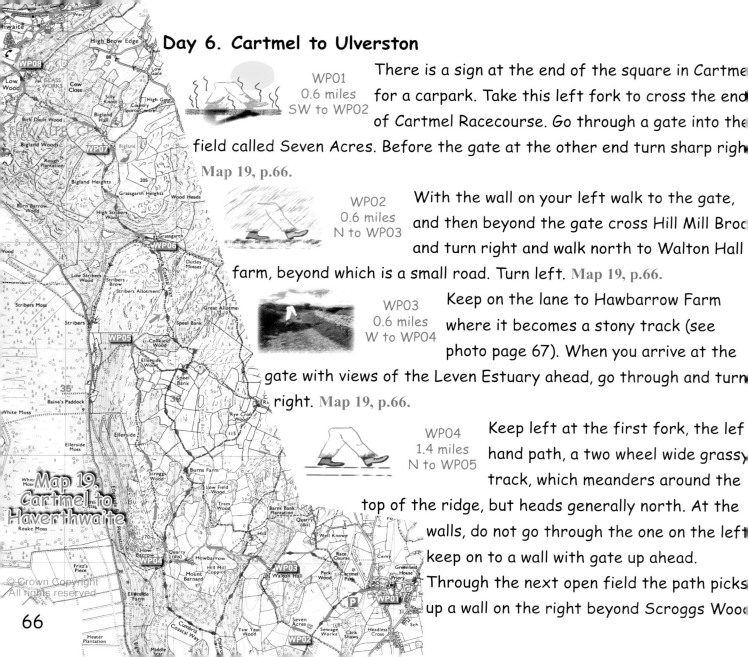

WP01
0.6 miles
SW to WP02

There is a sign at the end of the square in Cartmel for a carpark. Take this left fork to cross the end of Cartmel Racecourse. Go through a gate into the field called Seven Acres. Before the gate at the other end turn sharp right. Map 19, p.66.

WP02
0.6 miles
N to WP03

With the wall on your left walk to the gate, and then beyond the gate cross Hill Mill Brook and turn right and walk north to Walton Hall farm, beyond which is a small road. Turn left. Map 19, p.66.

WP03
0.6 miles
W to WP04

Keep on the lane to Hawbarrow Farm where it becomes a stony track (see photo page 67). When you arrive at the gate with views of the Leven Estuary ahead, go through and turn right. Map 19, p.66.

WP04
1.4 miles
N to WP05

Keep left at the first fork, the left hand path, a two wheel wide grassy track, which meanders around the top of the ridge, but heads generally north. At the walls, do not go through the one on the left keep on to a wall with gate up ahead. Through the next open field the path picks up a wall on the right beyond Scroggs Wood.

Towards How Barrow

Ellerside Ridge ←

Turn round
Collkield Wood →

67

Bigland Tarn

Through the next gate there is a wood on the other side of the right hand wall. Map 19, p.66.

WP05
0.7 miles
NE to WP06

Go through the gate (see photo page 67), at Collkield Wood onto a path that bears right round the wood and then rejoins the Cumbrian Coastal path. Look for a two way finger post in the middle of the field ahead. Turn left to Grassgarth. Map 19, p.66.

WP06
0.8 miles
NNW to WP07

Go through the gate onto the road at Grassgarth, turn right and immediately turn left through a small gate. The path drops down to a little footbridge. Up the other side bear left along the field to find a stile into Burn Barrow Wood. Leave the wood to cross the open ridge top until Bigland Tarn appears on the right. Map 19, p.66.

Angler's Arms, Haverthwaite

The bay near Canal Foot

WP07
0.8 miles
NW to WP08

Turn left, away from the lake edge and enter the woods again, rapidly descending to the road. Here turn right for a hundred yards to find the next left turn just before the road bridge. Map 19, p.66.

Lunch diversion
WP08 0.6 miles
back to WP08

If you feel like having lunch, there are two opportunities just up the road. There is the Angler's Arms pub at Haverthwaite which does good food, and there is a good cafe at the Haverthwaite Steam Railway Station just a few hundred yards beyond that (open Spring to Autumn). To get there from WP08 keep on the road, over the bridge and turn right onto a path across the field, this cuts off the corner to a building on the far side. Then right for a few hundred yards to find the pub. The cafe is a few hundred yards further on, over the busy A590 road. After lunch return to WP08. Map 19, p.66.

Haverthwaite Steam Railway

69

WP08
2.1 miles
W to WP09

This is a lovely flat path through to the footbridge at Greenodd. Over the bridge turn left and cross the road bridge and then left again down to the path which runs along the water's edge. **Map 20, p.71.**

WP09
3.6 miles
S to WP10

Walk south with the water on your left. At the left hand bend in the channel keep to the foreshore and follow it round in a right hand curve until you can see the railway viaduct south. There are a few gullies to cross, but the surface is marsh-grass, not mud and the gullies are not particularly challenging. **Map 20, p.70.**

WP10
0.8 miles
S to WP11

Turn right and follow the viaduct to a bridge under the railway line. Then walk round the edge of the next bay to arrive at Canal Foot and the Bay Horse Hotel. **Map 20, p.70.**

70 Swans on Ulverston Canal

Walkers' Hostel Ulverston

Map 20.
averthwaite to Ulverston

WP11
1.6 miles W
to WP12

Follow the canal up to the town of Ulverston. When you arrive at the road, the Walkers' Hostel is a few yards round to the right. Otherwise cross the road and head into the town. It is probably important to point out that after a short rest, wherever you are staying, it is a requirement to walk up the hill to the amazing lighthouse (Sir John Barrow's Monument) at the top. It can be done in the evening as an appetiser or tomorrow morning as it will be the only climb of the day. **Map 20, p.70.**

West Coast 19

Grassington 81

Ulverston Monument

Low Tide on Greenodd Sands

Hi-speed incoming tide

71

Day Seven
Terrain: Foreshore, flat as a pancake
(unless the sea to Piel Island is rough)
Distance: 16½ miles to Barrow via Rampside
(11 miles to Rampside, then either 5½ to Barrow, or 9 to Barrow via Walney)
Total Height Gain: 350 feet
Highest Point: (starting from 100 ft) 100 feet
Refreshment: Baycliff, Rampside, Roa Island

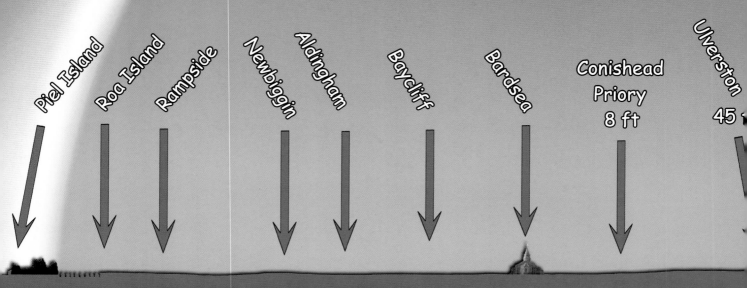

Piel Island
Roa Island
Rampside
Newbiggin
Aldingham
Baycliff
Bardsea
Conishead Priory
8 ft
Ulverston
45

Day Seven.
Ulverston to Piel Island
& Barrow-in-Furness

On the other side of the country, at end the *Grassington to East Coast Walk*, it is a good idea to stay an extra night in Robin Hood's Bay so that you have time to look round, before walking along the cliff to Whitby and then find your way home in a more relaxed manner. I think it is also very important to stay that extra night at the end of the *Grassington to West Coast Walk*. This is because you may want to take advantage of the extra walk described below - the walk over the sand to Walney from Piel Island. But even if you decide not to do that, it is important to take the ferry to Piel Island and have a look round. If you try to do all this on the same day you have walked from Ulverston, it will be a long day and probably not very successful. You have put a lot of effort into getting here, so it would be a pity not to relax and enjoy the success for at least another half day.

The route across the estuary sands from Piel Island to Walney Island, is discussed in more detail below. If you intend to follow this route you should only attempt it on an extra day. Don't be pressured and rush onto the sand - you need time to assess the route, confirm that you understand the tide times and only commit yourself when you are sure the conditions are right.

Across Morecambe Bay from near Aldingham

Day 7: Ulverston to Piel Island (& Barrow)

WP01
1 mile
S to WP02

Walk out of town and cross the main road to Barrow, the A590. The coast road, A5087 is sign posted for Bardsea. Keep on this road for half a mile after passing under a railway bridge. You will see The Old Farm House Restaurant on the right, and a cricket field on the left, just before the turn. The left turn is called West End Lane. Map 21, p.76.

WP02
1.2 miles
SW to WP03

300 yards after the turn there is a second turn onto Brick Kiln Road, a really pleasant single track road that leads to the estuary path. Look out for a brick built chimney and follow the road round right. Once on the coast look across the estuary for Chapel Island. It is the middle point of a route across the sand from Cark, but should only be attempted with a guide because it involves wading the river that is in front of you. Map 21, p.76.

WP03
1 mile
S to WP04

It is now slightly harder to get lost! Conishead Priory is in the woods to the right, and the path follows the boundary. It is a Buddhist Centre and open to the public (see informa-

Distant View of Piel Castle

75

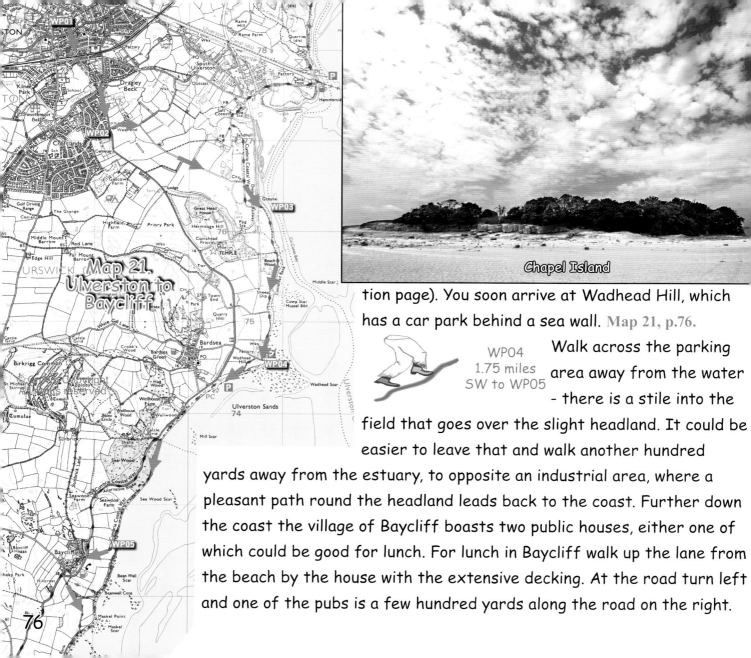

tion page). You soon arrive at Wadhead Hill, which has a car park behind a sea wall. **Map 21, p.76.**

WP04
1.75 miles
SW to WP05

Walk across the parking area away from the water - there is a stile into the field that goes over the slight headland. It could be easier to leave that and walk another hundred yards away from the estuary, to opposite an industrial area, where a pleasant path round the headland leads back to the coast. Further down the coast the village of Baycliff boasts two public houses, either one of which could be good for lunch. For lunch in Baycliff walk up the lane from the beach by the house with the extensive decking. At the road turn left and one of the pubs is a few hundred yards along the road on the right.

Chapel Island

Map 21,
Ulverston to
Baycliff

Map 22. Baycliff to Piel Island

(The other is in the village.) Return to the beach on a lane on the left a few hundred yards beyond the pub. Map 21, p.76.

WP05
3.7 miles
SW to WP06

Navigation is not difficult - there is a special prize for anyone who gets lost between here and Rampside.

The path is either shingle foreshore, grassy track or more substantial pavement and concrete sea wall. There are two pubs in Rampside and a very good cafe, the Bosun's Locker, near the end of the peninsula at Roa Island. Map 22, p.77.

WP06
1.5 mile
S to WP07
Piel Island

Roa Island used to be an island but was joined to the mainland by a railway line which was then converted to a road. So you can walk to the small wooden jetty from where the ferry plies backwards and forwards to Piel Island. The ferry is in view so you can see when it will be back and how many people are waiting to cross. I think it takes about 15 people for each crossing so it is small enough to get the feel of a proper boat trip, especially if it is windy and pleasantly choppy. The trip costs £3. Please note that the ferry only runs between Easter and October so during winter you either have to forgo a trip to Piel or hitch hike, which I managed to once (see below). If you are going to arrive here on a week day you can telephone John Cleasby (01524 701054) at least one day before you intend to get there and he will take you to the island by arrangement. Map 23, p.79.

Piel Island Ferry

House of many chimneys (12), Rampside.

The Clarke's Hotel & Pub

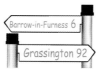

WP07
1.4 miles
N to WP08

Return to Roa, and walk back down the peninsula towards Rampside. **Map 23, p.79.**

WP08
1.5m
NW to WP09

The path leaves the road across a tarmac area just before you get to the Concle Inn (you could always ask for directions at the bar!). This leads behind the Concle Inn and becomes a fine wide track which, from the look of it, was probably the route of the railway line. This path returns to the edge of Roosecote Sands. On the way there are some wonderful views across the bay and also of a gleaming refinery on the right. **Map 23, p.79.**

WP09
1.7 miles
W to WP10
Barrow

At the end of the path, it turns left round a derelict warehouse and then right under a bridge to emerge on the edge of the town of Barrow. Turn left and follow the road to town. **Map 23, p.79.**

Lighthouse at Rampside

Map 23. Barrow via Roosecote Sands

Map 23. Barrow via Walney Island from Piel Island

The fine vessel Natlee & owner who very kindly gave me a lift to Piel Island

The Natlee

Barrow Town Hall on a bright and breezy day

Barrow in bloom

Lovely, shiny refinery

The Concle Inn, Rampside

Roosecote Sands Path

The Setting Sun - Piel Island

Alternative Route: across the sand from Piel to Walney Island. 9 miles (from Rampside).

This 'added extra' is most easily available on about twelve week-ends in the year when both ferry and low tide are in conjunction. However, the ferryman, John Cleasby, will agree to take you to the island if you telephone him at least one day before you wish to go, and if the weather is acceptable.

If that is the case and you have read and understood all the caveats that I list below, and still would like to 'nip' over the sand from Piel to Walney, you should stay an extra night and then catch the ferry to Piel so that you can calmly walk off the island onto the sand while the tide is still falling. Please note that I cannot recommend walking off the island onto Walney, even though it is an excellent way to end the walk. I have walked off that way myself, and by myself, and it is not in the 'immediate danger' category of many weekend pursuits, like potholing or cliff climbing. It is a more subtle danger, one that is hidden until over-confidence is established and then is suddenly upon you

It is also a very exposed experience feeling small on a vast slab of mud - and that is good. The danger of soft sand is something that cannot be planned for. If your feet start sinking what do you do? On a hill-top the tactic is to 'bog trot', run light and fleet-footed across the boggy bits until you get to drier tussocks. On a flat beach if you panic and run on carelessly, it may be that you run into even softer sand. The point is that you cannot see soft sand before you step on it. I have been told that sand with ripples is less likely to be soft than sand without ripples. I have also been told that the sand is softer in fresh water, so a rainy day could be a problem but it really means that wading across the fresh water flowing down the estuary could be dangerous. There are only a few little fresh water streams flowing off Walney into the Walney/Piel Channel.

Barrow-in-Furness 9

Grassington 92

A tactic that is comforting is to look for cars on Piel. The pub used to get all its supplies of beer etc., from a wagon that crossed the sand from Walney, and other people drive their cars across too. If a car is already there you can follow its tracks back to Walney knowing that you are going the right way. Do not take the fact that cars remain on the island as proof that you have time to walk across before the tide comes in — the owners of the cars may be camping on the island for a few days. Check the tide tables but unless you are very familiar with tides and tide tables you must get confirmation from someone who knows what they are talking about. It is too easy to read a tide table that is using GMT and then make the wrong calculation when adjusting to BST - is low tide and hour earlier or an hour later than GMT? I don't know either... but it could be the difference between Life and soggy socks!

John Cleasby, will tell you how much time you have before the tide returns. He will also analyse the weather conditions for you. If he said to me that the conditions or times were wrong, I would not go. Having said that, do not make John responsible for your actions, the choice is yours.

It is only 1½ miles from Piel to Walney but when you are out there it feels a lot further. However, the psychological experience still does not make the distance any greater. You could run across in half an

The causeway to Roa Island

hour. The other point in favour of this walk is that there are no major streams shedding water into the sands so there are no deep gullies. It is flat, open, exposed and very tempting. If you stick your neck out and get to the other side you will congratulate yourself for braving the elements, and perhaps, think that I have exaggerated the dangers. I do not think so. I have tried to explain that these sands become safer the more experience you have of them, and two walks across on good days, (the experience I have had) does not qualify me to assess all the dangers.

Don't park here!

 WP07
1.5 miles
W to WP08
Having made it to Piel Island you will find a pub, a row of houses and a castle plus quite a lot bird life. Have a look round unless time is too tight. If I haven't put you off yet, let's get onto the sand! Walk west past the row of houses to find where the track clearly drops off the island onto the flats. So now you have gone and done it, you are on the sand and walking away from dry land. You have to walk due west, so you need a

compass. You can see Walney Island all the way but that is not very useful if a bank of fog floats in from the sea. I have walked for a mile in very thick fog on top of Fountains Earth above Nidderdale, it seemed like three miles. It is called sensory depravation, your brain has nothing to process from one moment to the next so you begin to make things up. At least on the moor there were sprigs of heather and the occasional rock emerging from the murk. On the sand flats there would be no change for three quarters of an hour and you would begin to think that you are walking in circles. Do not go if you do not have a compass or a gps with good batteries. **Map 23, p.79.**

The road off Piel Island

Tracks across the sand

WP08
0.25 miles
W to WP09

Dry land, dry land.., this is Snab Point, you made it! What was all the fuss

bout? Just a little bit of sand and water. Valk off the sand onto a tarmac road, kiss he road... well, perhaps not. Turn right. his is Mawflatt Lane and you could follow directly to Biggar. However, round the rst bend there is a better route. Map 23, p.79.

WP09
1 mile
NW to WP10

There is a road up to the left which leads to the western side of Walney

with views like that on page 86/7. Turn right along the path between the foreshore and the fence. Map 23, p.79.

WP10
1.2 miles
NW to WP11

Take the path called Cow Leys Lane that leads to Biggar, and the

Queens Arms, a pub that serves good

food in very large portions. A suitable place to celebrate the achievement of having walked so far. Well done! **Map 23, p.79.**

WP11
1.4 miles
NE to WP12
After lunch it is better to walk back over to the western shore for the last mile or so. There is a path marked across Biggar Sands, which appears to cut the corner, but when I tried it I found there were many deep gullies,

which, had they been full of water, would have forced me to turn back. Instead, follow the western foreshore again as far as a right turn to Vickerstown. **Map 24, p.79.**

WP12
1.6 miles
NE to WP13
Barrow
Follow the road through Vickerstown to a left turn, beyond which is the bridge across into Barrow-in-Furness. Having arrived in Barrow, you will find plenty of things to

see, so it is a good idea to stay for a while. There is Furness Abbey just on the outskirts of the town. The famous shipping museum is close by. The town centre is like many other modern towns, which unfortunately means the same old names appear again and again, but then there is a comforting predictability about that. Map 23, p.79.

The Queen's Arms, Biggar

Due west from Walney Island

The red lines on the map on this page are the tracks recorded by my gps on the two walks I have completed across the sands between Piel and Walney. The blue and green arrows just show the direction I walked. The first walk followed the tracks of a vehicle that had driven over from Walney to Piel. At the time I did not notice Sheep

Birds at Walney

Island, but it is worth being aware of, because it is above high water mark and close to the edge of the marsh grass.

When I went to walk across again I found the ferry was temporarily out of action. I drove round to Walney and walked from there towards Piel Island. Hardly a quarter of a mile onto the sand and Piel Castle looked to be a couple of hundred yards further, but was still well over a mile away - distance is very hard to judge once you are on the sand. Because of the delay driving round I was concerned about the tide, even though it showed no sign of covering the sand I was walking on, so as I

Map 24. GPS tracks between Piel Island and Walney Island

approached Piel, I diverted to the far end of Walney Island, round Bass Pool and making for a derelict pier on the southern tip of Walney. There is a gully in front of the derelict pier where a stream flows from Walney into the sea, I crossed it without difficulty but had to walk upstream for a while to a narrower point. I could have waded but the thought of slimy mud slipping between my toes put me off. If you have a love of bird watching, this could be an exceptional extra day. The walk across

Piel Castle with Cumbrian Hills

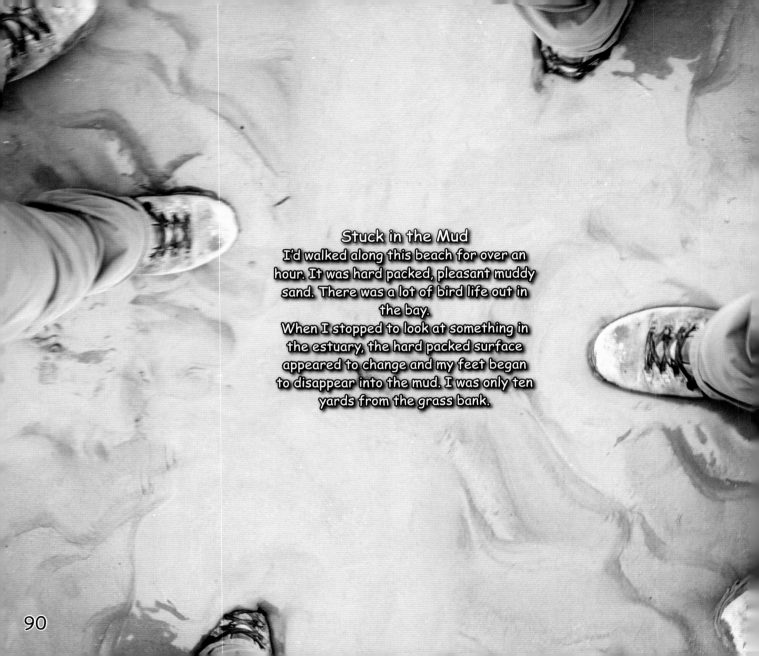

Stuck in the Mud

I'd walked along this beach for over an hour. It was hard packed, pleasant muddy sand. There was a lot of bird life out in the bay.

When I stopped to look at something in the estuary, the hard packed surface appeared to change and my feet began to disappear into the mud. I was only ten yards from the grass bank.

Piel Castle from South Walney

to the derelict pier) is only just over a mile, but then the walk round to Barrow is more like a further eight. haven't put in another alternative route because bird watchers are likely to wander around anyway. When was there the bird sanctuary was very noisy, there were several thousand birds shouting at me. I walked ound past the lighthouse and then had unrestricted views across Morecambe Bay, and could clearly see lackpool Tower in the distance. Once you leave the end of the island it is a wonderful foreshore walk as escribed above.

Accommodation

Please note that some of the tariffs listed are for twin/double rooms and some per person.

Grassington

The Foresters Arms, 20 Main Street, Grassington, Nr Skipton, N. Yorks. BD23 5AA. 01756 752349 (+44 1756 752349) www.yorkshirenet.co.uk/accgde/forestersarms/
Grove House, Guest House, 1 Moor Lane, Grassington. BD23 5BD 01756 -753364 www. grovehousegrassington.co.uk/grovehouse/
Scar Lodge Hardy Grange, Grassington, North Yorkshire, BD23 5AJ 01756 753388 val@grasssington.plus.co.uk www.yorkshirenet.co.uk/stayat/scarlodge/

Malham

Beck Hall, Alice Maufe, Cove Road, Malham. North Yorkshire. BD23 4DJ 01729-830332 alice@beckhallmalham.com

Settle

The Golden Lion Hotel Philip Longrigg, Duke Street, Settle, North Yorkshire BD24 9DU

01729 822203 (+44 1729 822203) 01729 824103 (+44 1729 824103) info@goldenlion.yorks.net

The Oast Guesthouse, 5 Pen-y-ghent View, Settle, North Yorkshire BD24 9JJ. 01729 822989 (+44 1729 822989) king@oast2000.freeserve.co.uk

http://www.yorkshirenet.co.uk/stayat/theoast/

page1.asp

Clapham

Arbutus Guest House. Riverside, Clapham, (Nr Settle), North Yorkshire, LA2 8DS. Tel. +44 (0) 15242 51240

http://arbutus.co.uk/contact.html

The Old Manor House Licensed Bunkhouse Accommodation, Clean, comfortable and afford-able. www.claphambunk.com/services.html

Ingleton

Bridge End Guest House. Mill Lane, Ingleton, North Yorkshire LA6 3EP. A lovely location beside the river in the village. Full facilities including a vegetarian menu, drying room, meals, packed lunches. All rooms en suite with TV. Bed and breakfast from £24 per person per night. Tel: 015242 41413 (+44 15242 41413)

Kirkby Lonsdale

Copper Kettle Guest House , 3-5 Market St, Kirkby, Kirkby Lonsdale. Cumbria. LA6 2AU

Silverdale

Challan Hall. Silverdale, Lancashire, LA5 0UH Tel/Fax : 01524 701054 E-mail: cas-sons@btopenworld.com http://www.challan-hall.co.uk/index.html

The Silverdale Hotel, Shore Road, Silverdale. Carnforth, LA5 0TP. Tel: 01524 702258. B&B £45 single, £75 per room for twin or double. http://www.thesilverdalehotel.co.uk/

Cartmel

Bank Court Cottage, The Square, Cartmel, Grange-over-Sands, Cumbria, LA11 6QB. Tel : 015395 36593

Priors Yeat, Pat & Charles Rowsell, Aynsome Road Cartmel, Grange-over-Sands. LA11 6PR
Tel: 01539 535178
priorsyeat@hotmail.com

The Cavendish Arms, Cartmel, Cumbria, LA11 6QA
T: 015395 36240 - info@thecavendisharms.co.uk
www.thecavendisharms.co.uk

Haverthwaite

The Coach House, B&B, Hollow Oak, Haverthwaite, Cumbria, England, LA12 8AD. Tel: +44 (0)15395 31622 E-Mail: coachho@talk21.com http://www. otinternet.com/~coachho/

Ulverston

The Walker's Hostel, Oubas Hill, Ulverston, Cumbria. LA12 7LB. www.walkershostel.co.uk/
Tel/Fax: +44(0)1229 585588
Email: info@walkershostel.co.uk

The Walker's Hostel provides low budget accommodation in a family run environment and is an ideal place for walkers to base themselves to discover the delights of the English Lake District or experience the carnival atmosphere of Ulverston, the birthplace of Stan Laurel.

The hostel is open throughout the year and has 30 beds in 7 rooms, ranging from 2 singles in a room to 7 singles in a room. There is also a family room containing a double bed, 2 singles and a cot.

Rampside

Clarke's Hotel, Rampside, Barrow in Furness. Cumbria. LA13 0PX. 01229 820303. Prices from: £79 to £95 per room b&b.

Roa Island

Roa Island Guest House, Piel Street, Barrow in Furness, Cumbria. LA13 0QL 01229 822525

Roa Island House is an imposing and unique 19th century guest house situated on the water's edge of Morecambe Bay near Barrow in Furness. Non smoking throughout, the house enjoys expansive sea views and retains much of the charm and elegance of Edwardian times. We offer a warm, relaxed, informal and friendly atmosphere away from the hustle and bustle. Tariff from £25 per person.

Barrow-in-Furness

East Mount House 55 East Mount, Abbey Road, Barrow in Furness. Cumbria. LA13 9AD
01229 871003. East Mount House guesthouse is beautifully decorated and appointed. Seven delightful bedrooms are available to guests, all with exquisite co-ordinated linen and furnishings. Tariff £24 - £27 per person B&B.

Places of Interest

Conishead Priory House & Temple Tours. Weekends and Bank Holidays from Easter to end of October 2007 (except during festivals) Tours begin at 2.30pm and 3.45pm. Adults £2.50, Children £1.50, Senior Citizens and unemployed £1.50 Conservatory Cafe. Open weekends & Bank Holidays at the following times (except during festivals) 2.00pm - 5.00pm Easter to end of October 2007

Leighton Moss an RSPB reserve of shallow meres, reed beds and salt marsh, famous for its rare, yet accessible, birds and other wildlife. Leighton Moss is the largest remaining reed bed in north-west England. The reserve is well-known for its special birds: breeding Bitterns, Bearded Tits, Marsh Harriers and Avocets. Opening times: The reserve and visitor centre are open daily all year round (except 25 December). The reserve is open from 9 am to dusk and the visitor centre from 9.30 am-5 pm (4.30 pm November-January inclusive). Entrance charges: Free to the visitor centre and tearoom. Admission to hides and nature trails: £4.50 adults, £3 concessions, £1 children, £9 family.

Holker Hall & Gardens. Cark-in-Cartmel, Nr Grange-over-Sands, Cumbria. LA11 7PL. tel: 015395 58328. The Hall, Gardens and Lakeland Motor Museum comprise of three spectacular attractions in a perfect setting.

The Laurel & Hardy Museum, 4c Upper Brook Street, Ulverston. Cumbria. LA12 7BQ http://www.laurel-and-hardy-museum.co.uk/

Lakeside & Haverthwaite Railway Co. Ltd, Haverthwaite Station, Nr Ulverston. Cumbria. LA12 8AL Tel: 015395 31594 Take a steam train from Haverthwaite and twenty minutes later you are at the southern tip of Lake Windermere where a large boat waits to take you up the lake as far as you like, to Bowness or Ambleside. Have lunch, look around and then return. Fares including a cruise on Windermere Haverthwaite to Bowness. Adult Return £12.60.

South Walney Lighthouse & Piel Castle

Piel Castle from on the sand